Searchlight
BOOKS

Getting into Government

Exploring the

Executive
Branch

Barbara Krasner

Lerner Publications ◆ Minneapolis

Lerner Publications
An imprint of Lerner Publishing Group, Inc.
241 First Avenue North
Minneapolis, MN 55401 USA

For reading levels and more information, look up this title at www.lernerbooks.com.

Main body text set in Adrianna Regular.
Typeface provided by Chank.

Library of Congress Cataloging-in-Publication Data

Names: Krasner, Barbara, author.
Title: Exploring the executive branch / Barbara Krasner.
Description: Minneapolis : Lerner Publications, [2020] | Series: Searchlight books. Getting into government | Includes bibliographical references and index.
Identifiers: LCCN 2018059308 (print) | LCCN 2019005147 (ebook) | ISBN 9781541556799 (eb pdf) | ISBN 9781541555891 (lib. bdg. : alk. paper) | ISBN 9781541574786 (pbk. : alk. paper)
Subjects: LCSH: Presidents—United States—Juvenile literature. | Executive departments—United States—Juvenile literature.
Classification: LCC JK517 (ebook) | LCC JK517 .K73 2020 (print) | DDC 351.73—dc23

LC record available at https://lccn.loc.gov/2018059308

Manufactured in the United States of America
1-46045-43367-4/2/2019

Contents

Chapter 1

THE EXECUTIVE BRANCH

During his first full week in office in January 2017, President Donald Trump signed several executive orders. One order aimed to speed up environmental approvals for large projects such as highways. President Trump said that getting these projects done quickly would help the US economy. The US Constitution gave the president the power to issue executive orders.

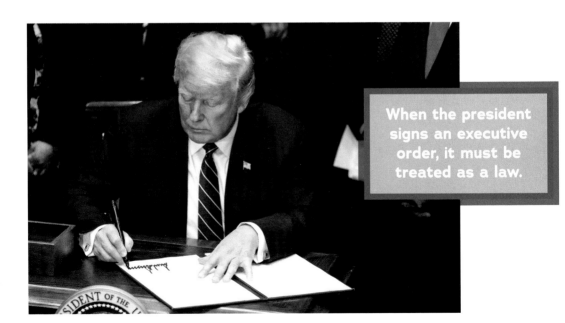

When the president signs an executive order, it must be treated as a law.

That's a Fact!

Franklin Delano Roosevelt signed 3,721 orders. One order in 1933 introduced the New Deal. It helped Americans during the Great Depression (1929–1942) by creating more jobs. Abraham Lincoln issued an executive order in 1863 that eventually freed slaves in the South. It was called the Emancipation Proclamation. Dwight Eisenhower's order in 1957 sent federal troops to Little Rock, Arkansas. The troops enforced a law that said black students and white students could attend the same schools.

President Eisenhower used an executive order to send troops to Little Rock Central High School.

Three Branches

The US government has three branches: the executive, legislative, and judicial. The Constitution defines the responsibilities of each branch. The branches work together to make laws for citizens to follow.

The Founding Fathers gave the US government three equal branches.

IF CONGRESS HAS ENOUGH VOTES, IT CAN OVERRIDE THE PRESIDENT'S VETO.

The main job of the executive branch is to carry out laws. The president leads this branch. The president signs laws written by Congress in the legislative branch. The president can also veto, or stop, a bill that Congress has passed. Congress has two parts: the Senate and the House of Representatives.

The White House holds just a small part of the executive branch.

The vice president works for the president. He also presides over the Senate during ceremonial events, and he can cast a tiebreaker vote. The vice president takes over as president if the president can't finish the term.

The executive branch includes other groups that help carry out laws. One group is the president's cabinet. Executive departments and federal agencies help as well.

One Leader, Many Roles

The president has many roles. The president influences how the country manages its money. Another role is to advise on how to control inflation, or how quickly prices rise. The president represents the United States to the world and meets with foreign leaders.

President Barack Obama speaks with Prime Minister Yingluck Shinawatra of Thailand.

The president must work with both the legislative and judicial branches to make decisions. The founders of the country wrote the Constitution this way. They didn't want one branch of government to have too much power.

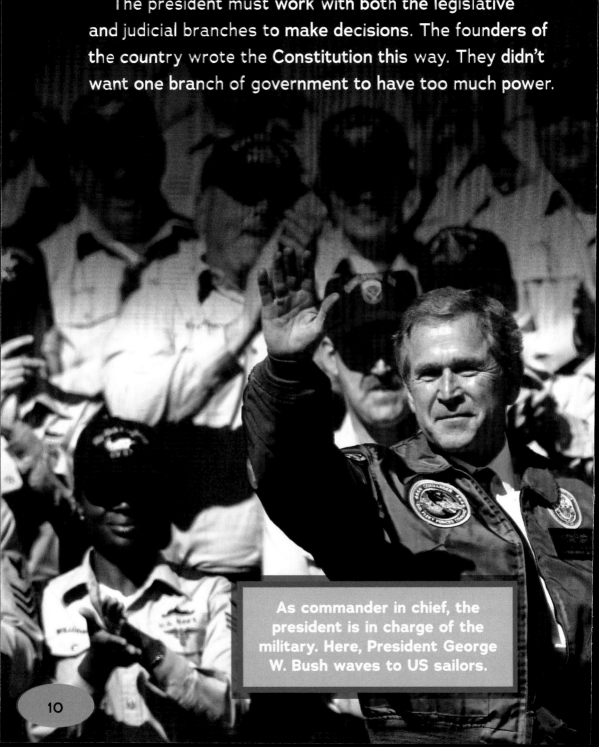

As commander in chief, the president is in charge of the military. Here, President George W. Bush waves to US sailors.

Chapter 2

LEADING THE COUNTRY

The Constitution lays out requirements for presidents to be elected. A president must have been born in the United States. The president must be at least thirty-five years old.

Congress limits the number of years a president can be in office. The president's term is four years. The

president can serve two terms. The vice president is also elected to a term of four years. But vice presidents can serve any number of years and under different presidents.

George Clinton was the vice president for both Thomas Jefferson and James Madison.

A Trusted Team

To fulfill his duties, the president needs the help of other people. These people should be experts in their fields. The president chooses them carefully. One important leader is the White House chief of staff. This person manages the executive office.

PRESIDENT RONALD REAGAN MEETS
WITH DIFFERENT EXPERTS.

Nikki Haley was President Trump's first ambassador to the United Nations.

When a new president enters office, a new administration enters too. The president chooses candidates for the administration. The president appoints US ambassadors to serve in other countries. The president also appoints federal judges and justices of the Supreme Court. All these appointments require the Senate's approval.

Government Affects You

In July 2018, the US Supreme Court heard an important case. The case was called *Juliana v. the United States*. Twenty-one children and young adults filed a lawsuit against the federal government. The lawsuit said the government had helped cause climate change. It argued that this violated the children's constitutional rights to life, liberty, and property.

Kids organize to make their voices heard in government.

Chapter 3

ADVISING THE PRESIDENT

The Constitution set up the executive cabinet. These people help the president make decisions. The idea of a cabinet dates back to George Washington's presidency. Then there were only three executive departments: State, War, and the Treasury. These days, the cabinet has fifteen different departments! They all perform specific duties. The cabinet also includes the vice president and the attorney general.

A president's cabinet includes the leaders, or secretaries, of each executive department.

Frances Perkins was the first female cabinet member. President Franklin D. Roosevelt appointed her.

The head of each department is the secretary. The president calls on secretaries for their opinions on important issues. One example is the secretary of state. This secretary advises the president and carries out foreign policy. In 2017, the secretary of state visited more than thirty countries.

Protecting Resources

The secretary of the treasury helps the president with economic affairs. The department includes the Bureau of Engraving and Printing and the US Mint. The US Mint designs and produces money. Alexander Hamilton was the first secretary of the treasury.

Did you know the executive branch is in charge of printing money?

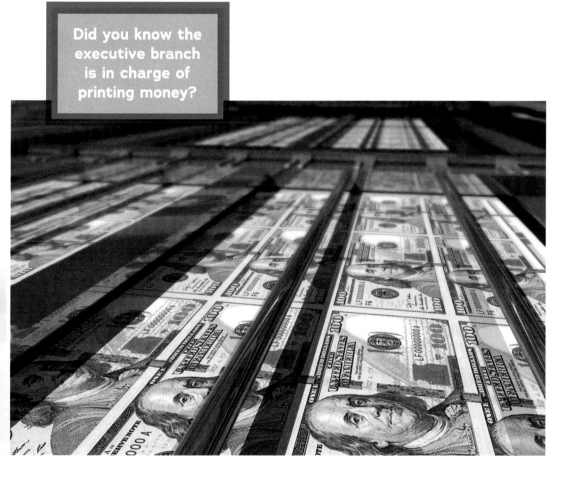

The Department of the Interior protects the United States' natural resources. The National Park Service is part of this department. It formed in 1916. The country has more than four hundred national parks.

Another part of the Department of the Interior is the Bureau of Indian Affairs. It works for the interests of American Indian peoples.

The Department of the Interior manages the land in the national parks.

Staying Safe

Some cabinet departments protect the United States. The secretary of defense oversees the military. The military has five branches. The army is the oldest and largest. The navy and the marine corps were created in 1775. The newest branches are the coast guard and the air force.

Secretary of Defense Chuck Hagel speaks to troops in 2014.

The government checks everyone who enters the US from another country.

The Department of Homeland Security protects the United States from outside threats. It monitors the country's borders. This department is also in charge of immigration policies. An informal office of homeland security formed in 2001. It formed just days after terrorists attacked the United States on September 11. This office officially became the Department of Homeland Security in 2003.

Government Affects You

The secretary of education advises the president on decisions about schools. One decision was the No Child Left Behind Act. President George W. Bush signed it into law in 2002. The government had noticed that some children got a better education than others did. The goal of the No Child Left Behind Act was to give every child a good education. The act set up standardized tests to measure schools' success.

Presidents can sign laws that change what happens in schools. How else does the government affect you?

21

Chapter 4

EXECUTIVE WORK

Hundreds of agencies and commissions do the executive branch's work. They help apply the department secretaries' decisions to daily life.

The CIA is one agency helping the executive branch do its work.

Protecting the Country

One of these agencies is the Central Intelligence Agency (CIA). Its role is to collect information. The agency learns about threats to the United States. It takes direction from the president.

Another agency is the Environmental Protection Agency (EPA). Its job is to protect the environment. This agency creates rules for people and companies to keep the air, land, and water clean.

Sometimes EPA employees test water to see if it's clean.

The National Archives and Records Administration manages presidential libraries. It also preserves US government records. It takes special care of the United States' founding documents. The Declaration of Independence, the Constitution, and the Bill of Rights are on display in the National Archives Museum in Washington, DC.

The Constitution created the US government.

Research at universities often leads to new discoveries in fields like astronomy.

Progress in Science and Peace

The National Science Foundation was formed in 1950. It helps fund important research at American colleges and universities. Their findings promote scientific progress.

Peace Corps volunteers learn what a community needs and help to accomplish it.

Peace Corps volunteers travel to other countries. They help with education, health, and training. The idea for this agency came in 1960. Massachusetts senator John F. Kennedy spoke at the University of Michigan. He asked ten thousand students if they were willing to serve their country in the name of peace. Many said yes. As president, Kennedy signed the Peace Corps into action in 1961.

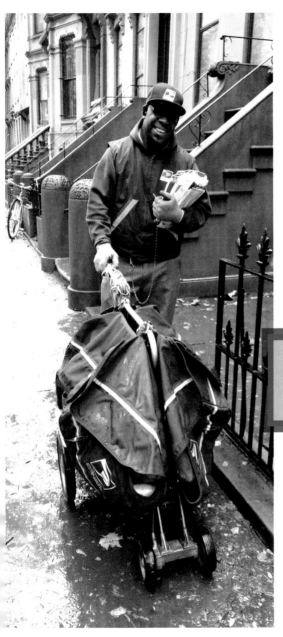

Mail Delivery

The US Postal Service delivers mail to your home. The Postal Service's mission is to provide fast and affordable mail service. Mail gets delivered, no matter where people live.

Postal Service employees deliver mail in every kind of weather.

That's a Fact!

The Federal Emergency Management Agency was formed in 1979. Its goal is to give aid when a disaster strikes. The agency is under a lot of pressure. Some people believe it did not do enough to help after Hurricane Harvey. The hurricane damaged parts of Texas and other southern states in 2017.

When a disaster happens, it's important to respond quickly.

Who's Right?

In 1947, Congress limited the number of terms for a president to two. But some experts believe the president needs more time to make important changes. During a crisis, the country may need to keep the same president longer. It could help the country's leadership stay steady.

But too many terms could give the president too much power. It could result in a dictatorship. The Constitution put in place checks and balances. These help maintain the country's democracy.

Do you think the president should only serve two terms? Why or why not?

Franklin D. Roosevelt was elected four times.

Glossary

administration: the people working in the executive branch under a president

bill: a draft of a proposed law

cabinet: the president's group of advisers

commission: a group of people with a specific job

dictatorship: a nation or state controlled by one person

executive order: an order signed by the president that must be treated like a law

inflation: a rise in prices and loss of the value of money

policy: a set of rules about what should be done

term: a set period an elected official is allowed to serve

veto: to reject a bill

Learn More about the Executive Branch

Books

Bausum, Ann. *Our Country's Presidents: A Complete Encyclopedia of the U.S. Presidency.* Washington, DC: National Geographic, 2017.
Learn about each of the forty-three former presidents of the United States.

Buchanan, Shelly. *Our Government: The Three Branches.* Huntington Beach, CA: Teacher Created Materials, 2015.
Find out how the executive, legislative, and judicial branches work together.

Higgins, Nadia. *US Government through Infographics.* Minneapolis: Lerner Publications, 2015.
Explore the government's three branches and the Constitution through fun graphics.

Websites

Ben's Guide to the US Government
https://bensguide.gpo.gov/
Explore the US government with an animated Ben Franklin as your guide.

Central Intelligence Agency: Kids' Zone
https://www.cia.gov/kids-page/
Play games and learn more about how intelligence for national security helps the president carry out executive duties.

Executive Command
https://www.brainpop.com/games/executivecommand/
This game lets you step into the president's shoes and try to achieve your policy goals.

Index

Photo Acknowledgments

Image credits: Oliver Contreras/SIPA USA via AP Images, p. 4; Bettmann/Getty Images, pp. 5, 29; ZU 09/DigitalVision Vectors/Getty Images, p. 6; Alex Wong/Getty Images, p. 7; vichie81/Shutterstock.com, p. 8; Jack Kurtz/Getty Images, p. 9; Chris Livingston/Getty Images, p. 10; bauhaus1000/DigitalVision Vectors/Getty Images, p. 11; Courtesy Ronald Reagan Library, p. 12; MA and F Collection 2018/Alamy Stock Photo, p. 13; Robin Loznak/ZUMA Press, Inc./Alamy Stock Photo, p. 14; Pete Souza/The White House, p. 15; Keystone-France/Gamma-Keystone/Getty Images, p. 16; altamira83/iStock/Getty Images, p. 17; Matt Anderson Photography/Moment/Getty Images, p. 18; Pool/Getty Images, p. 19; Christopher Morris/Corbis/Getty Images, p. 20; PAUL J. RICHARDS/AFP/Getty Images, p. 21; SAUL LOEB/AFP/Getty Images, p. 22; Win McNamee/Getty Images, p. 23; spatuletail/Shutterstock.com, p. 24; Hero Images/Getty Images, p. 25; AP Photo/Pablo Aneli, p. 26; Keith Getter/Moment Mobile/Getty Images, p. 27; NICHOLAS KAMM/AFP/Getty Images, p. 28.

Cover: Official White House Photo by Shealah Craighead.